I am so grateful  comfort that flows from this devotional. Laurie Pauls and Laura Laskowski, what you have done through these pages, courageously sharing glimpses of your own personal motherhood moments, is uniquely beautiful. *Draw Near* takes you on a sacred journey, revealing the joys and sorrows of a mother's love and ultimately leaving your soul refreshed with steadfast hope grounded in Jesus and His Word. Reading this devotional has significantly impacted and inspired me to see, in fresh ways, how God is refining my heart through the gift of being a mother to my sweet girls and seeing that my strength comes when I *draw near*.

—Ruth Anne Durance
mother of two little girls

Laurie and Laura share their motherhood journeys from hearts that have been transformed by God's love. Their personal stories, refreshing honesty, and insight bring hope and encouragement to others. I have watched God use them in our community and it's so exciting to know that many more will have the opportunity to be encouraged and blessed through this book. I'm sure this is only the beginning for Laurie and Laura!

—Maureen Brown
mother of three children by birth and three by marriage
grandmother of three boys
Family Ministry Pastor, Forest Grove Community Church

Wonder–full! *Draw Near* introduces Laura and Laurie, two moms who are real in their honesty, unassuming in their wisdom, and deep in their awareness of God's presence in the laundry and logistics of a mother's life. Their simple yet poignant reflections will reorient you into the wonder and awe of who God is and His attentiveness amid the complex emotions of motherhood. Let yourself laugh, then linger with these nourishing words from two newfound companions on your faith journey.

—Leanne Schellenberg
mother of two teenagers
Spiritual Formation Practitioner

The spirit-filled devotionals are equally applicable to both men and women. They were a source of blessing and encouragement to us.

—Clarence and Elaine Koop
parents of two adult sons and their wives
grandparents of three

30 Devotions of
Hope for Moms

LAURA LASKOWSKI
& LAURIE PAULS

DRAW NEAR
Copyright © 2020 by Laura Laskowski & Laurie Pauls

All rights reserved. Neither this publication nor any part of this publication may be reproduced or transmitted in any form or by any means, electronic or mechanical, including photocopying, recording or any information storage and retrieval system, without permission in writing from the author.

"A Mother's Love" cover painting by Martie Giesbrecht.

Unless otherwise indicated, all Scripture quotations are taken from the Holy Bible, New Living Translation, copyright © 1996, 2004, 2015 by Tyndale House Foundation. Used by permission of Tyndale House Publishers, a Division of Tyndale House Ministries, Carol Stream, Illinois 60188. All rights reserved. The Holy Bible, English Standard Version (ESV) is adapted from the Revised Standard Version of the Bible, copyright Division of Christian Education of the National Council of the Churches of Christ in the U.S.A. All rights reserved. Scripture quotations marked (NKJV) taken from the New King James Version®. Copyright © 1982 by Thomas Nelson. Used by permission. All rights reserved. Scripture quotations marked (NIV) are taken from the Holy Bible, New International Version®, NIV®. Copyright © 1973, 1978, 1984, 2011 by Biblica, Inc.™ Used by permission of Zondervan. All rights reserved worldwide. www.zondervan.com The "NIV" and "New International Version" are trademarks registered in the United States Patent and Trademark Office by Biblica, Inc.™ Scripture quotations marked MSG are taken from THE MESSAGE, copyright © 1993, 2002, 2018 by Eugene H. Peterson. Used by permission of NavPress. All rights reserved. Represented by Tyndale House Publishers, a Division of Tyndale House Ministries.

Printed in Canada

Print ISBN: 978-1-4866-1890-3
eBook ISBN: 978-1-4866-1891-0

Word Alive Press
119 De Baets Street, Winnipeg, MB R2J 3R9
www.wordalivepress.ca

Cataloguing in Publication may be obtained through Library and Archives Canada

I dedicate this book to my daughters, Kaylin Rain and Raya Josie. You are the Rain and Raya sunshine God is using to help me grow. I will love you forever and ever, no matter what!

—Laurie

I'm so excited to dedicate this first book to my husband Kevin, who has lovingly read all the random devotional "moments" I've written in the last decade and encouraged me to keep writing. Also to my three awesome, funny, creative, and always-teaching-me kids: Olivia, Ashlyn, and Alex.

But above all, I dedicate this to my amazing heavenly Father who speaks to me, whispers to me, and guides me in all the crazy I am. He's my stable rock in this roller coaster called life.

—Laura

Contents

	Acknowledgements	ix
	Dear Mamas	xiii
1.	Daily Life Maintenance–Read Psalm 139	1
2.	Be Still–Read Psalm 46	3
3.	Search for Significance–Read Jeremiah 18:1–6	6
4.	Perfect Love–Read 1 John 4:7–21	9
5.	Lessons in the Laundry–Read Proverbs 16:20	11
6.	Praise: How I Fight My Battles–Read Isaiah 61:1–11	13
7.	Respect–Read Ephesians 5:21–33	16
8.	Mission Homefront–Read Jeremiah 29:11–13	18
9.	Resurrection–Read Philippians 3:1–14	21
10.	The Beauty of the Valley–Read Psalm 121	24
11.	Joy of the Lord–Read Nehemiah 8:1–12	26
12.	Grace and Honesty–Read Ephesians 4:29–32	28
13.	Roll Up Your Sleeves–Read 1 Peter 1:1–21	30
14.	Mushrooms–Read 2 Chronicles 16:9, Psalm 116:1–2	32
15.	Wisdom–Read Proverbs 1:1–7, 4:18–23	35

16.	Grace to the Humble–Read 1 Peter 5:5–11	37
17.	Life with Margin–Read Ephesians 5:15–17	39
18.	Be Real–Read Deuteronomy 31:6–8	42
19.	Making Allowance–Read Colossians 3:1–17	45
20.	The Butterfly–Read Genesis 1:26–2:7	47
21.	Rescue Plan–Read Jonah 2:1–10	49
22.	Maximizing Our Differences–Read Romans 12:1–16	52
23.	Ski Lesson–Read Psalm 18:28–32	55
24.	He Chose–Read Hebrews 12:1–3, Philippians 2:1–11	58
25.	Twinkle, Twinkle, Big, Big Star–Read Isaiah 40:28–31	61
26.	Your Will Be Done–Read Matthew 6:7–13	63
27.	Broken for You–Read Jonah 4	65
28.	The Oasis–Read John 4:1–26	67
29.	Laughing Ladies–Read Proverbs 31:10–31	70
30.	Our Life Mosaic–Read Psalm 5:1–12	73
	An Invitation	77
	About the Authors	79

Acknowledgements

God: Thank you for being our teacher, guide, helper, and the reason we have hope, joy, and peace—and something to write.

Husbands: Thank you for your consistent love and support in both our daily lives and this new writing adventure. We couldn't do it without you.

Kids: Thank you for teaching us what true love requires and really is… and for the generous grace you have extended to us as we learn and grow alongside you.

Marge and Dale Warkentin: Thank you for taking the time to sit with my devotionals over your morning breakfast and give helpful feedback. Thank you, Mom, for the hours you spent editing my writing. More importantly, though, thank you for your steady example of a healthy marriage and teaching me how to draw near to God all these years.—Laurie

Elmer and Shirley Thiessen: Thank you for raising me in a warm and loving home and family that had faith in Jesus as its foundation. Thank you also for consistently encouraging me over the years in my unique personality and gifting. It gave me room to explore this area of writing. As an adult, I am so thankful for your visits to our house and our long, meaningful chats over a strong cup of coffee… mmm, good.—Laura

Tamara and Trevor Smith: Thank you first for being so loving and caring in my life as my sister and brother-in-law. Secondly, thank you for taking the time to edit these devotionals for our first printing, giving helpful feedback, and prodding me along on this writing venture.—Laura

Tracey Thiessen: Thank you for being a mentor to me over my years of marriage and mothering (ever since you married my brother Mark). Thank you also for cheerleading me as I wrote these devotionals and being another set of eyes.—Laura

Brad Berken: Thank you for giving us opportunities to explore our gifts of writing and helping us bring the writings together beautifully to give to the moms at our local church.

Martie Giesbrecht: Thank you for reading our devotionals and allowing the Holy Spirit to move through your art, providing us with the beautiful cover to our book, which inspired the title. (Martie can be contacted at martieg@sasktel.net)

Grace Fox: Thank you for being my first writing mentor and gently teaching, encouraging, and affirming me to both grow in my writing and keep on writing. I am forever grateful for the beautiful godly foundation for writing that you taught and modelled to me.—Laura

Sylvia St. Cyr: Thank you for believing in this devotional and helping us to see that it is worth publishing.

Leanne Deobald: Thank you for sharing your excitement and photography talents with us by taking our headshots.

Evan Braun: Thank you for your faithful attention to detail as you edited and polished our manuscript.

Marina Reis: Thank you for walking us through the process of publishing our first book.

Laura: Thank you for listening to the Holy Spirit and getting us started on this writing project. I treasure your gracious encouragement, prayers, and friendship.—Laurie

Laurie: All I can say is that I am completely amazed at how God has directed me to you for a writing teammate. I am so thankful for how God has gifted you with the perfect personality complement to me for writing. You are such a blessing as both a close friend and now a co-writer. Thank you for all you do to keep us organized and for your beautiful gift of writing.—Laura

Draw near to God, and he will draw near to you.
—James 4:8a (ESV)

Dear Mamas,

We just wanted to say a warm hello and thank you for taking time out of your full and busy lives as moms to read the little moments of learning and inspiration we share in the following pages.

We are fellow sojourners on this path of motherhood who are imperfect, have good days and hard days, and learn a lot along the way. Our prayer in opening our hearts through writing is to encourage you and share about how having a life with Jesus brings hope and freedom in the everyday challenges of our own identity, marriages, and parenting.

We ourselves know the need to be continually reminded of truths God has taught us through scripture and life's circumstances. We are praying that what we've learned will help you as well.

> *May God give you more and more grace and peace as you grow in your knowledge of God and Jesus our Lord.*
> —2 Peter 1:2

Now pour yourself a warm cup of coffee, tea, or hot chocolate and be blessed as you read.

one

Daily Life Maintenance
Read Psalm 139

By Laura Laskowski

Today I was determined to write. I sat down at my computer and couldn't focus. All around me was clutter, dust, and to-do lists. It was overwhelming.

Laundry piles were waiting in the laundry room—I had done most of the laundry on the weekend but left two small loads. I had managed to get the kitchen chaos cleaned up by the end of the morning, but still all this other stuff was yet to be done.

Aarghh! The daily grind of life and mess and busyness over and over and over was getting to me. What should I do?!

Knowing that I wouldn't be able to write well with chaos around me, I decided to spend some time writing a few emails (the pressing ones), dusting (specifically the computer desk and the room it's in), sweeping (the main crumbs and dust), and starting a load of laundry. Then I felt like I could breathe and actually gather my thoughts.

Life is like that. Without time to maintain the basics in our homes and families, we can quickly start to feel stress and chaos. Babies, school-aged children, husbands, work schedules, unexpected issues, and all the regular day-to-day cooking, dishes, and dirty laundry can very easily drive us to a point of insanity.

In the last few weeks, I admit, I've been teetering on the edge. And if I'm not careful to create some margin in my life, I know I'll start taking this out on those I love and care about most—my husband and my kids.

So here are a couple of the things I know from past experience but need to remind myself of and relearn often: God made me, and God gave me the ability to know Him and know myself.

I need *time* to be reminded of these two very important things. If I'm running around constantly like a crazy chicken mama with her head cut off, I will forget. So I need time to be quiet and remember who I am and what I can handle. Time to listen to God and be in His presence will renew and refresh me.

I also need time to maintain the basics of my home and family. God has blessed me with a home, a husband, and three children—and I need to be a good steward of all of these. If my life outside the home doesn't allow me enough time and space to take care of myself and spend time with God, if it doesn't allow me enough time to take care of my home and family, something has got to change.

As I pray the Serenity Prayer over me and my family, I hope you pray it too: "God, grant me the serenity to accept what I cannot change, the courage to change the things I can, and the wisdom to know the difference."

two

Be Still

Read Psalm 46

By Laurie Pauls

Be still, and know that I am God! I will be honored by every nation. I will be honored throughout the world.
—Psalm 46:10

THERE IS ALWAYS SOMETHING ELSE THAT COULD BE DONE around the home—another teachable moment with the kids, another load of laundry, another nutritious meal to prepare, something out of our control that we are desperately trying to solve. There are so many things we should be doing! So much falls on our shoulders! We think, *If I don't do this, who will?*

Into our stress, busyness, and worry is this command: "Be still, and know that I am God!"

In the middle of the night this week, I was praying desperately about something I wanted control over. It was causing me anxiety but was completely out of my control. This was something I wanted God's help with.

I prayed around in circles for a while and then this verse—*"Be still, and know that I am God"*—broke into my thoughts. It came to me like a loving and gentle *shhhh* from the Holy Spirit. My breathing slowed and deepened as my mind meditated on that truth before falling back to sleep.

My spirit could be still.

God heard my prayer, my desperation. Now my job was to be still and trust that He is God. How to answer my prayer was up to Him. I needed to open my hands and release it to Him, to lay down my unknowns, my hopes, and my worries at His feet and enjoy sleep again. What will be is His will and I need to trust in His love for me, no matter the outcome.

God welcomes our prayers, including our desires about things outside our control. We aren't expected to hold our whole world together, and He loves it when we open our hands to entrust it all to Him. As we put our trust in His goodness and sovereignty, we receive peace that surpasses all understanding.

This year, God has given me a picture of Him as a big daddy lion—and I am a lion cub. I am His beloved and precious child. No matter the trouble I face in this life, I am the cub and I have my big daddy Lion to snuggle up to in the darkness. He will carry me on His back when I face overwhelming circumstances. I am not expected to be full-grown, but instead I can trust Him to be the King of the jungle.

> *Don't worry about anything; instead, pray about everything. Tell God what you need, and thank him for all he has done. Then you will experience God's peace, which*

exceeds anything we can understand. His peace will guard your hearts and minds as you live in Christ Jesus.
—Philippians 4:6–7

Listen to the Song:
"Build My Life," by Pat Barrett.

three

Search for Significance
Read Jeremiah 18:1–6

By Laura Laskowski

When I was thirteen years old, I remember babysitting for a young family. It was one of my first longer babysitting jobs, as it lasted a full day—from morning until late at night. My job was to take care of a two-and-a-half-year-old. No problem, I figured. I was the fourth child in a family of six kids, so I knew all about taking care of kids.

Well, maybe not.

This little girl was in the midst of potty training. Yes, I'm sure you can imagine my day of "learning." A few hours in and this little sweet girl had made a big mess in her underwear. I honestly didn't know what to do. You don't keep the underwear, do you?! That's disgusting, I thought.

So how did I solve this dilemma? Well, no joke, when the little toddler was napping I took the pair of underwear and walked to the back of the yard, dug a hole just beyond the fence with the little sandbox shovel, and buried the dirty underwear.

It's crazy to think I actually did that! Obviously, I had a *lot* to learn about babysitting.

Since becoming a mother, I've often thought back on that incident. It's been a humbling reminder that in so many ways I haven't had a clue how to be a mother. Mothering has been a very challenging journey for me, yet one that has pushed me to be far more open and vulnerable to needing God.

In my early years of being a mom, I read *Search for Significance: Seeing Your True Worth through God's Eyes*, by Robert S. McGee.[1] It took me about a year to very slowly read through it. It was completely what I needed for God to gently nurture my hurting, broken spirit. I had been in a place where I felt like I wasn't a good mom or a good wife. The enemy was wreaking havoc on my mind and heart in my long days at home. Negative thoughts consistently whirled around my head, and soon I was believing these lies.

It was *very* hard work to teach myself to think differently, but slowly and gradually I learned to allow God to mould me. He became my Potter—not the world, not my mind, not my performance as a wife or mother—but, simply and purely, God.

> *Then I went down to the potter's house, and there he was, making something at the wheel. And the vessel that he made of clay was marred in the hand of the potter; so he*

---

[1] Robert S. McGee, *Search for Significance: Seeing Your True Worth through God's Eyes* (Nashville, TN: W Publishing Group, 2013).

made it again into another vessel, as it seemed good to the potter to make.

—Jeremiah 18:3, NKJV

I could *not* have made it through those years without God's work in my mind and heart.

Today I continue to need Him to mould me and gently or firmly remind me that His thoughts of love and significance are what I need above anything or anyone else.

I pray you will go to God in your hurt, in your lack of feeling capable, in your days of wanting to bury the dirty underwear, and allow Him to be your potter. You are worth it.

Listen to the Song:
"You Say," by Lauren Daigle.

four

Perfect Love

Read 1 John 4:7–21

By Laurie Pauls

I HAD A LOVE/HATE RELATIONSHIP WITH 1 JOHN 4:18—"*There is no fear in love. But perfect love drives out fear, because fear has to do with punishment. The one who fears is not made perfect in love*" (NIV).

I love that there's a place where there is no fear. Perfect loves drives out fear. When fear is absent, there is room for peace, hope, and joy. This is freedom and the full life Jesus said He came to bring: "*I have come that they may have life, and have it to the full*" (John 10:10, NIV)

However, many times I've felt like I haven't measured up because I was still experiencing fear. I believed I was doing something wrong when fear gripped my body and spirit. On top of fear, my thoughts spiralled into thinking that my faith must be weak, that I hadn't done enough in my Christian life. I had been fed the lie that I wasn't good enough.

As fear swept me away, my next thought would be that I still hadn't figured it out. I was not yet made perfect in love.

One day while driving on the highway by myself, a song came on the worship playlist I was listening to, and a line jumped out to me about my fears being drowned in perfect love. Somehow this helped me understand 1 John 4:18 in a whole new light.

It's not that I have to be perfect or arrive at a mysterious place to be set free; it's that God is love and God is perfect. Therefore, God's love is perfect and He is worthy of our trust. I can surrender and release control even through the fire and storms, through the unknowns and heartbreaks. I can trust that He is loving me perfectly even when I don't understand or like what's going on around me.

He is still at work. He is still good. He is still loving me perfectly.

It's true—trusting in His perfect love drowns my fears. The next time fear grips our chest, may it be the trigger that causes us to turn to the One worthy of our trust.

Listen to the Songs:
"No Longer Slaves," by Bethel,
and "Sovereign Over Us," by Shane & Shane.

five

Lessons in the Laundry
Read Proverbs 16:20

By Laura Laskowski

Several years ago, I remember a significant moment when God showed me that He can speak very directly through the mundane tasks of my daily life. It was midmorning and I was at home with my two daughters. My girls were around the ages of five and two, and I was trying to keep an eye on them while folding laundry at the kitchen table. It was a very typical day of doing housework and being a mom, nothing different or special about it.

As I was getting to the bottom of the basket of laundry, I saw a book. I didn't know how or when it had gotten there, but very likely one of the girls had put it in there at some point and all the laundry had gotten piled on top of it.

It wasn't just any book. It was a soft plush book called "All About Me," with my older daughter's picture in the front picture pocket. It had been a baby gift for her, and we had filled it with significant photos of her as a little girl and baby. She loved looking through it.

Well, what's the big deal? A book at the bottom of the laundry basket? Nothing so exciting about that.

But it stopped me. This was God's way of speaking very directly to me about how He wanted to speak life and encouragement to me in the daily grind. He had not forgotten about me. In the middle of my laundry, He was there.

It was also a challenge for me to make sure I don't let the "laundry" of life bury and overwhelm me. Good things can take up space in my life, and I need to give these things to God. But the *dirty* laundry of life—things from my past, personal failures, hurts, negative thoughts—can also bury me and cause me to forget who I am and whose I am: God's child.

So I write this to encourage you in your daily grind, to help you take notice of the ways in which God is trying to speak to you—and it's often in a whisper.

Numerous times since then, God has been very creative in speaking to me. He's so good at connecting with each of us in ways we can understand.

But there is a catch—we have to be open and we have to be trusting. His voice won't carry through a brick wall easily. God doesn't force us to hear Him. He will speak, but the choice to listen and hear it is ours.

I pray you will find your own lesson in the laundry today, however God creatively speaks to you. Let's make sure we are listening. Have an amazing day, no matter how typical it is!

six

Praise: How I Fight My Battles
Read Isaiah 61:1–11

By Laurie Pauls

> *The Spirit of the Sovereign Lord is on me, because the Lord has anointed me to proclaim good news to the poor. He has sent me to bind up the brokenhearted, to proclaim freedom for the captives and release from darkness for the prisoners, to proclaim the year of the Lord's favor and the day of vengeance of our God, to comfort all who mourn, and provide for those who grieve in Zion—to bestow on them a crown of beauty instead of ashes, the oil of joy instead of mourning, and a garment of praise instead of a spirit of despair.*
>
> —Isaiah 61:1–3, NIV

MOTHERHOOD HAS BEEN THE MOST CHALLENGING AND wonderful journey of my life. My daughters are the sunshine and rain that have forced growth upon me.

When my girls were young, I found myself in a dark and rainy season, teetering on the edge of depression, anxiety, and despair. I didn't want to stay in that dark place.

Into my darkness came the book *1000 Gifts* by Ann Voskamp.[2] I inhaled it. I found a journal and started recording all the things I was thankful for.

Through the days filled with fear and discouragement, I started looking for God's goodness and claiming it as His love for me. I was on a search for rays of sunshine breaking through.

My senses were opened to enjoy small things—the giggle of my baby, the smell of lilacs along the sidewalk, a toddler chasing bubbles with wonder, the touch of a little hand reaching for mine... and writing these tiny moments down allowed me to savour them, and to believe in God's great love for me, helping turn me from a spirit of despair to a spirit of praise. Honestly, this was the beginning of my journey towards freedom and a full life in Jesus.

Miracles happen in our lives when we practice gratitude. Hope breaks through the clouds. Trust in God strengthens our roots. Peace falls like rain. Joy sprouts and flourishes.

I was disciplined and wrote more than ten things I was thankful for each day until I had filled a couple journals. I kept going until it was incorporated naturally into my thought patterns, prayers, and the way I experienced each day.

I don't write down my gifts much anymore, but I receive them, enjoy them, and praise God for all the ways He expresses His love for me.

---

2   Ann Voskamp, *1000 Gifts* (Grand Rapids, MI: Zondervan, 2010).

Draw Near

As moms, we're fighting spiritual battles in our own lives, in the lives of our children, and in our marriages. We need something to remind us that when it looks like we're surrounded on every side, we are also surrounded by God. Let His love and gifts remind you that you're not fighting all the challenges alone. This is how we fight our battles, mamas!

Therefore, let us offer through Jesus a continual sacrifice of praise to God, proclaiming our allegiance to his name.
—Hebrews 13:15

Listen to the Song:
"Surrounded (Fight My Battles)," by Michael W. Smith.

seven

Respect

Read Ephesians 5:21–33

By Laurie Pauls

…and the wife must respect her husband.
—Ephesians 5:33

I believe that the commands in the Bible instructing wives to submit and respect their husbands were written because these aren't things that come easily to us. It takes intentionality, effort, learning, and transformation by the Holy Spirit to submit to and respect our husbands.

For more than a decade of marriage, I really struggled with disrespectful thoughts toward my husband. My husband isn't perfect, but he was definitely not deserving of disrespect. I held it in as best I could, but of course it came out in words and actions on a regular basis. Luke 6:45 explains it well: *"What you say flows from what is in your heart."*

I sought the Lord about my struggle, and eventually I was ready to hear that my need for control was at the root of my disrespectful thoughts. Any time my husband acted outside of what I wanted him to be doing, negative thoughts and emotions were triggered in me. Being a person who tried to control almost everything around me, you can imagine how often this happened!

As the Lord is teaching me to submit to Him, He is also helping me to release my control and submit to my husband. It becomes much easier to respect my husband when I'm not trying to control him. As I've gotten the hang of this, I have experienced mental and emotional freedom. And maybe for the first time in our fifteen years of marriage, I'm no longer plagued by negative thoughts toward my husband. I can purely enjoy him as the person God created.

Changing our natural reactions to situations doesn't happen overnight. But I believe with the power of the Holy Spirit and lots of opportunity to practice, experiencing victories and failures, these reactions and thought patterns can be transformed.

For God is working in you, giving you the desire and the power to do what pleases him.
—Philippians 2:13

Listen to the Song:
"The Hardest Art," by Switchfoot.

eight

Mission Homefront

Read Jeremiah 29:11–13

By Laura Laskowski

A FEW YEARS AGO FOR CHRISTMAS, MY DAUGHTER GAVE ME A trendy decorative pillow for our couch. She knows I love positive quotes, encouraging verses, and things around our house with words on them that remind me of the important things in life. Ever since I opened this present that Christmas Eve, the pillow hasn't left the couch in our main living space.

Well, it has been on the floor many times, but at least it remains in the same room.

Needless to say, the words on this pillow have helped me define my role as a mom. The pillow reads, very simply, "Home is where your story begins." Nothing more, nothing less. Since receiving the pillow, I've noticed this phrase on many home decor items in stores, on calendars, etc. I imagine you've likely seen it, too.

Even though this is a very simple and somewhat obvious little sentence, with deeper thought and insight God has used it to help me focus on what is important in my life as a mom, as a wife, as a woman, and as a person who desires to contribute to my home, community, and beyond.

So much so, in fact, that a few years ago I wrote a three-evening seminar series for young moms to share what God had been placing on my heart. I called it "Mission Homefront."

Here I will give you the main ideas behind what God highlighted to me. I call it the *circle of priorities*.

The very centre circle, being the core of our priorities, is ourselves. You could put your own name in the middle. Now, this doesn't mean we are egocentric. The opposite actually. It means we are making sure that we know our identity well so that we can give our best to the next priorities.

Also within that circle, and most important, is knowing our identity as God's child, His very treasured daughter. By knowing that and having God at the centre of who we are, having a genuine relationship with Him, we will make wise decisions on how to be and how to do life. Our roots will be grounded in the right thing.

The next circle, which goes around the core circle, is our relationship with our husbands. This is not the core circle, because in order to have a healthy marriage relationship we need to know ourselves well and place our identity in God, not our husbands.

With this circle, we need to make sure we make it a priority to take care of our marriage relationship. If things in the core circle are falling apart, likely things in this circle are also crumbling. Watch for this and don't ignore the root things that need to be addressed.

In the third circle, which encircles the other two, are our children and home environment. Notice that children are not the number one priority, as much as society seems to push this. And a clean house is not the number one priority, as much as it feels like it should be at times.

Nonetheless, the priority of our children and home environment is more important than our jobs, our extended family, or our close friends. And again, if the other two circles mentioned earlier are cared for, we can do a much better job of taking care of our kids and home.

Now, what does any of this have to do with the phrase "Home is where your story begins"? Well, I've found that if I can base my decisions on this circle of priorities, I will take care of my homefront.

Ultimately, for myself, my husband, and my kids, home is where our story begins… and if we can for the most part keep those core priorities at the forefront, we will succeed. God will give us the wisdom and grace to do well. Our homes and families will be blessed, and from there we can go out and conquer the world!

nine

Resurrection

Read Philippians 3:1–14

By Laurie Pauls

Much of my energy, time, and resources are spent trying to avoid suffering for myself and those I love. I use a variety of vitamins, essential oils, and cleaning products to avoid or minimize the effects of sicknesses that come our way. As a mom, I teach my kids about potential dangers and how to be careful.

I am unable to quantify the amount of emotional energy I've used up over the years worrying about things that just might happen. I'm certain that if it was possible to calculate it, the amount would be staggering.

It is in our nature to avoid pain and suffering as much as possible. But as we all come to understand early on in life, a lot of suffering is unavoidable. No matter how many times I wash my hands, trying to avoid germs, I inevitably get sick. Even though I worry about the physical safety of my kids, they injure themselves whether I'm absent or present.

I'm also aware that there is much greater suffering in the world than a common virus or skinned knee. I only need to turn on the news or listen to someone's life story to hear of the devastations that happen in our community and around the world.

Paul challenges me greatly in Philippians 3:10–11 when he writes,

I want to know Christ and experience the mighty power that raised him from the dead. I want to suffer with him, sharing in his death, so that one way or another I will experience the resurrection from the dead!

For those things in our lives that cause us to suffer physically, mentally, and emotionally, we can pray for healing, for a miracle. That is good, okay, and normal.

But while we wait for the answer, we can find hope and patience in Paul's perspective. As we suffer, we can get to know Christ better, share in His death, and experience new life.

I know I pray for physical healing more than spiritual healing, but God is more concerned with the state of our hearts and our faith than our physical comfort.

Therefore, since we have been justified through faith, we have peace with God through our Lord Jesus Christ, through whom we have gained access by faith into this grace in which we now stand. And we boast in the hope of the glory of God. Not only so, but we also glory in our sufferings, because we know that suffering produces perseverance; perseverance, character; and character, hope.
—Romans 5:1–4, NIV

Draw Near

I'm beginning to understand that through times of suffering, suffering I either couldn't imagine or wouldn't choose, new life and hope is being born. This is resurrection.

Listen to the Song:
"Resurrecting," by Elevation Worship.

ten

The Beauty of the Valley

Read Psalm 121

By Laura Laskowski

LIFE IS HARD; LIFE CAN BE HARD; LIFE WILL BE HARD.

Life was maybe hard for you in childhood, it may be hard in adulthood, or it might be hard sometime down the road. But when you're going through the *hard*, know that God has purpose in it and will use it for His good in your life—*if* you choose to allow God to do that. That's a big *if*. We can choose to allow hard stuff to refine, shape, and cause us to grow, or we can get angry, bitter, and choose to allow it to harden our hearts.

Someone gave me a beautiful vision to focus on when I find life extremely hard. In this image, there are two mountain peaks, both of them grand and majestic. Yet in the middle of these two peaks is a valley. Initially, the valley looks unimportant and dull. But if you take a closer, deeper look, the valley is green, full of growth, and contains a river where the trees are receiving life. It's a rich, lush valley even though at the outset, between the majestic mountains, it looks insignificant.

This picture has given me great encouragement time and time again. It has reminded me of the beautiful growth that can happen during our most challenging times in life. Looking back on those times in my life, I can definitely attest to that.

It doesn't feel good going through the valley months and years of my life. However, during those times I lean heavily into God and He is so faithful to use those challenging times to cause growth in me. He causes me to dig deep into the river of my soul, which reveals my ugliness, my faults, and my shame and allows Him to bring newness out of them. He has brought forth new growth and new life out of really hard stuff.

Psalm 121 gives glory to God. It's also a good reminder that as I seek Him for my help, He will be faithful to me, day and night.

I encourage you to write Psalm 121 down somewhere so you can refer to it often. May it be an inspiration to keep trusting God when you're going through the valleys of growth. May it remind you to thank God when you're experiencing the mountaintops. It's also a powerful psalm to pray over your children.

> *I will lift up my eyes to the hills—From whence comes my help? My help comes from the Lord, who made heaven and earth.*
>
> —Psalm 121:1–2, NKJV

eleven

Joy of the Lord

Read Nehemiah 8:1–12

By Laurie Pauls

…for the joy of the Lord is your strength.
—Nehemiah 8:10, NKJV

I knew this commonly quoted verse for a long time before I learned where it came from in the Bible. For the longest time, I also understood it to mean that experiencing joy makes us stronger. I had also learned that joy comes from the Lord, as it says in Galatians 5:22: *"But the Holy Spirit produces this kind of fruit in our lives: love, joy, peace, patience, kindness, goodness, faithfulness, gentleness, and self-control. There is no law against these things!"*

When I was at my darkest point with two young kids, I was desperate for joy and for the strength it would bring. I was searching and asking for this gift of joy.

I found that practicing gratitude increased my feelings of joy and led me to feeling more hopeful. This did strengthen me for the journey of motherhood, with its major ups and downs.

Finding things to be thankful for on those really hard days proved to be incredibly helpful and encouraging. It helped me to see that moments of joy are possible, no matter the circumstances.

This kind of joy was something I had to fight for, to search for. It came and left with my shifting perspective on life; sometimes I would feel thankful, other times I'd feel sorry for myself.

Last spring, a friend wrote me an email, causing me to understand this verse in a whole new light:

> I have found it to be very helpful to spend dedicated time in prayer praising God for who He is instead of thanking Him for what He has done for me. For me, this has helped take my eyes off of the circumstances I'm in and bask in the greatness of God.

As I read the email, my mind went to this verse and suddenly expanded my understanding: the joy of the Lord is in *who* He is. We can find incredible strength in focusing on who He is, leading us to experience lasting joy in who He is as well. Our emotions, circumstances, and the people around us are always changing, but He was and is and will always stay the same. Who God is can be the steadfast source of our joy and strength.

In addition to being thankful for the moments laughing with our kids, the warm sunshine on our face, or a quiet space to sip hot coffee, we can praise and thank God for being gracious, wise, powerful, the source of all creativity, redeeming, patient, faithful, generous, perfect, loving, unchanging, and…

May the joy of the Lord—*who* He is—be our strength!

Listen to the Song:
"Joy of the Lord," by Rend Collective.

twelve

Grace and Honesty

Read Ephesians 4:29–32

By Laurie Pauls

One evening last year, I was mad at my husband about something and wasn't sure how to handle the situation. I can't remember what it was about anymore, but I do remember that while walking my dog I asked the Lord how I should talk to my husband about it. I clearly heard God say to me, "Grace and honesty."

That evening, I walked thirty minutes instead of the five I had planned, so I could think about those two words and the importance of the order in which they had been given to me. First, God was asking me to look at my husband and the conflict between us with a heart of grace. Once that was in place, room was created for being honest.

But if I was only honest, I would end up being the one in need of grace.

The words grace and honesty pop into my mind regularly. At first they seem simple and easy enough. I quickly realized that I'm much better at the honesty part, but I have a ton of learning to do in the grace department. My natural reaction when someone brings out hard emotions in me is to blame, resent, question their intentions, and blow things up. Slowly but surely, God is helping me replace blame and anger with grace.

The first step in replacing blame with grace is to acknowledge this tendency and desire to respond with grace, rather than to react out of anger. We are not expected to do this perfectly on our own strength. If we turn our eyes toward God when we find ourselves in a familiar pattern of reaction, the Holy Spirit can begin to transform us and show us a new way forward.

When I have hard feelings, I wonder if it's a self-pity reaction, something I shouldn't be feeling. Sometimes this is the case, but sometimes it's not. When God said I could be honest, when preceded by grace, I felt like He was validating my feelings. He was saying that I could give them space to exist, to be expressed with grace, and then allow them to pass on by. I have found that when grace takes the lead in our communication, the negative feelings really do move on, and I experience freedom rather than self-pity.

Let's be pioneers as we allow grace to show us a new way forward—out of our old patterns and into uncharted territories of love.

Listen to the Song:
"Pioneers," by For King & Country.

thirteen

Roll Up Your Sleeves

Read 1 Peter 1:1–21

By Laura Laskowski

My patience gets most tested within the walls of my home. As much as I try to make my home a place of refuge, a place of warmth and kindness, a place of love and forgiveness, I'm often the one to wreak havoc. Being a mom is crazy hard. It's my first place to do missions—and sometimes the hardest place.

I love this verse plopped in the middle of the first chapter of Peter's letter to those Christians facing persecution: *"Therefore gird up the loins of your mind, be sober, and rest your hope fully upon the grace that is to be brought to you at the revelation of Jesus Christ"* (1 Peter 1:13, NKJV).

Satan is a very real enemy who will persecute us relentlessly. He makes his persecution so personal and specifically designed to each of us that we don't even recognize it's him. Maybe it's a comment made on Facebook, an image on Instagram, a passing statement from your husband, or a frustrating day with the kids. Satan knows these things can tear down our walls of faith if we aren't careful. And that's exactly his plan.

The same verse, and the ones following, written in The Message read:

Draw Near

So roll up your sleeves, put your mind in gear, be totally ready to receive the gift that's coming when Jesus arrives. Don't lazily slip back into those old grooves of evil, doing just what you feel like doing. You didn't know any better then; you do now. As obedient children, let yourselves be pulled into a way of life shaped by God's life, a life energetic and blazing with holiness.

—1 Peter 1:13–16, MSG

These verses tell me:

1. Get ready to work. (Satan is always at work, and so must we in order to keep our guards up).
2. Use the gift of your mind to think wisely.
3. Be ready for Jesus at all times.
4. Don't be tempted to go back to old, sinful ways.
5. Allow God to shape you and you will be *"a life energetic and blazing with holiness."*

Today, choose one area where the enemy is tripping you up and make an intentional choice to quit doing it. Ask for God's strength and guidance in deciding how you will accomplish this. Then ask a close friend or family member to keep you accountable.

…but as He who called you is holy, you also be holy in all your conduct…

—1 Peter 1:15 NKJV

fourteen

Mushrooms

Read 2 Chronicles 16:9, Psalm 116:1–2

By Laura Laskowski

While walking around my yard this morning, I was stopped in my tracks by a huge mushroom. It didn't literally block my path, as it was in the middle of the yard, but it was big enough to make me stop and take notice—probably five inches in diameter and three inches tall, bright white against the green backdrop of grass.

After a brief moment of looking at it, I continued on my way.

But when I later thought on its significance, tears came to my eyes. The good kind of tears, sad but happy.[3] The past weekend, mushrooms had come up as a topic of conversation several times. A strange topic to discuss, you think? Perhaps.

Grandpa, my husband's grandfather, went to meet his Saviour last Wednesday. And what a man he was. A man of God, a man of integrity, a man of love and great generosity, a very hardworking businessman, a former town mayor of forty years, an

---

[3] My kids are always bewildered by this type of tears. "How can you cry and yet be happy at the same time?"

incredible father, husband, and grandpa. He lived life in the fast lane and to the fullest. He walked quickly and was passionate about everything he did. As he would say, "Life is no Mickey Mouse operation."

But even though Grandpa lived life to the fullest, he knew when to stop and take notice of something—and one very significant way in which he did this was by picking mushrooms.

One day, his truck was discovered on the side of a road, pulled over into the ditch, and no one knew where he had gone. Well, after some searching he was found deep in the bush, picking mushrooms. These mushrooms were fried in butter that evening for a delicious addition to supper.

He picked mushrooms to share and enjoy many, many times, and he knew from childhood which ones were safe to eat and which were not.

Mushrooms were one way in which God got him to slow down. God knew that mushrooms got his attention and helped him to enjoy creation, to breathe deeply, to walk slowly, and likely to release stress. Picking mushrooms was so enjoyable for Grandpa that he would go searching for them. He didn't just find them right where he was walking; he would take time away from everything else to go look for them.

This reminds me of Jesus. Despite the very hectic life and ministry He lived on a day-to-day basis, He searched for times of quiet in creation and in the presence of God. These were the experiences that made Jesus an effective leader, teacher, and friend.

I think the same was true for Grandpa.

Which explains the sad, happy tears I shed when I saw that mushroom in my backyard.

It's amazing how God can minister to me so deeply through a simple mushroom. Thank You, God, for putting that right in my path. Next time, I think I might just head into the bush searching for mushrooms. And thank you, Grandpa, for being a powerful example of living a life committed to Jesus.

Watch for the special and specific ways in which God is ministering to you today—and then go after it! He'll give you what He knows you need. Record it in a journal, or on a list on your fridge or mirror. You'll be so encouraged that He loves you and wants to minister to you extravagantly, even if it's in the simplest of ways.

fifteen

Wisdom

Read Proverbs 1:1–7, 4:18–23

By Laurie Pauls

Guard your heart above all else, for it determines the course of your life.

—Proverbs 4:23

Proverbs 4:23 is a very common and familiar verse. It can be found on posters, bookmarks, and journals. Many people know it without even trying to memorize it.

I've been a Christian all my life but have never quite understood how I was supposed to guard my heart. Does it mean putting up certain types of boundaries or walls, keeping some things at a distance? Does it mean being careful with what I expose myself to seeing and hearing? Does it mean I shouldn't give my love to just anyone?

As I read through the book of Proverbs this winter, the writer kept repeating how valuable wisdom is, such as in Proverbs 3:15: *"Wisdom is more precious than rubies; nothing you desire can compare with her."*

While repeating this verse, I began to understand that the way to guard my heart is by growing in wisdom. Proverbs 9:10

says, *"Fear of the Lord is the foundation of wisdom. Knowledge of the Holy One results in good judgment."* This clarified and simplified things for me. I guard my heart by growing in wisdom, and I grow in wisdom by humbling myself before the Lord.

More than studying, reading, and gleaning knowledge from others to grow in wisdom, we need to remember who we are in relation to the God of the universe. Anything that humbles us is a gift because from a place of humility we can better understand our need for God in our lives and receive His help and wisdom. When we're humble, we're open to discipline, to learning, to listening to Him and following His ways. When we follow His ways, our hearts are guarded and He can determine the course for our lives. This will always be the best way forward.

Just as most kids struggle to trust our good intentions when we discipline them, it's easy to doubt God's love and good intentions when we're disciplined. We resist, talk back, blame others, and experience fear. When this happens, may we also learn to humble ourselves before God and allow Him to determine the course for our lives.

Listen to the Song:
"The Strength to Let Go," by Switchfoot.

sixteen

Grace to the Humble

Read 1 Peter 5:5–11

By Laurie Pauls

And all of you, dress yourselves in humility as you relate to one another, for "God opposes the proud but gives grace to the humble."

—1 Peter 5:5

MY FRIENDS AND I OFTEN SHARE ABOUT THE DRAMA THAT happens in our families just before leaving for church on Sunday mornings. Fifteen minutes before we leave becomes the most frantic time in our week. We're quickly finishing up breakfast, brushing through knots in long blond hair, brushing teeth while looking for something that has gone missing, and one or more of us is angry and/or losing our minds.

This past Sunday, I tore a strip off my family as we were racing to put our shoes on—and I almost swore. I almost said the sh-word, but I modified it so it wasn't the real thing. Yikes.

I sat silently during the car ride to church and felt quite humble. I sure needed church. I needed to apologize. I needed grace. I needed more of Jesus.

I went to church fully aware of my needs and that I didn't have it all together.

I've often wondered if the fifteen minutes of drama before church has something to do with attacks from the evil one. Maybe he was trying to discourage us or trip us up, causing us to arrive late.

But as I drove to church with a fresh understanding of my need for more of God, I began to wonder if God opposed me so I would arrive at church dressed in humility. Maybe it's better for me to come in a state of recognizing my humanness and need for His grace instead of feeling proud, like I had it all together on my own.

Being dressed in humility doesn't feel very good, but I have to say that as I sat in the pew that morning I listened intently. My heart was ready to receive more of God and the grace He gives.

I hope that the next time emotions are elevated and we're frantically trying to get our families to church on time, we can remember that in the chaos of it all, we are being dressed in humility. And this is a very good thing.

> *And he gives grace generously. As the Scriptures say, "God opposes the proud but gives grace to the humble." So humble yourselves before God. Resist the devil, and he will flee from you. Come close to God, and God will come close to you.*
>
> —James 4:6–8 (emphasis added)

Listen to the Song:
"Power to Redeem," by Lauren Daigle.

seventeen

Life with Margin
Read Ephesians 5:15–17

By Laura Laskowski

"I'm going to lose it!" I yelled.

Once again, my kids argued with me and each other as I pushed them out the door. With one hand, I carried my eight-month-old son in his car seat. With the other, I tried to grab everything my daughters needed for school.

"Hurry up! Hurry up!"

The pressure pot of my patience boiled over.

This is so stressful, I thought repeatedly. *But this is your lot in life, so get used to it.*

Our family's move to an acreage brought with it the commitment to drive the kids to school. Granted, a school bus stopped at the end of our driveway, but using its services meant switching from the city school to a rural one. I hadn't wanted to do that. Why should I? A friend I highly respected nearby had driven her kids to the city school for years.

I would do the same. I'd have to. Doing otherwise would mark me as a failure. Or so I thought.

I can do this! I told myself daily despite the stress it caused me and my kids.

A year passed before I grew desperate enough to re-evaluate. I felt like I had no margin in my life. Something had to change.

As a stay-at-home mom, I find it difficult to create and protect margin in my life. Perhaps you can relate: household chores, driving kids to school or extracurriculars, volunteering at church or in the community, and subconsciously trying to meet other's expectations can consume us. If we're not careful to put margins in our lives, we can easily become resentful of our role.

So here are four things I've done to protect my margins, and in doing so become a happier mom.

1. Seek God. Keep it simple. Try reading a devotional, meditating on a particular verse, or reading the Bible for five minutes per day. Say a short prayer, inviting God into the mundane of your day while running errands. Listen to worship music while doing housework. If we seek God daily, He will help us make wise decisions about how to use our time and set boundaries to eliminate stress.

2. Review your schedule monthly. How's it working for you and your family? Are adjustments needed? If so, what will they look like, and how will making them alleviate stress? I do this regularly now, and I'm always pleasantly surprised to see how God brings clarity to my life.

3. Say no, even though many of us find it difficult. We say yes too many times for a variety of reasons—we know we're capable of fulfilling the request, we're afraid to say no, we don't know our limits—and eventually we pay a price. On the flip side, maintaining margin by saying no leaves white space and gives us time to recharge, play with our kids without feeling a time crunch,

and enjoy unexpected blessings. Strangely enough, I've discovered that most people actually respect those who say no, if it's done in a loving and respectful way.

4. Don't compare. God created each of us differently. My amount of margin will differ from other moms. That's okay. As I recognize and appreciate how God made me, I become a more confident decision-maker about my needs and those of my family without falling into the comparison trap.

After a few months of intentional reflection and prayer, my husband and I chose to send our kids to the rural school. They now hop on and off the bus at the end of our driveway. This decision created margin in my life and alleviated stress for everyone. Now they're happier, and so am I.

eighteen

Be Real

Read Deuteronomy 31:6–8

By Laura Laskowski

Our culture works hard to cover up reality. We want to portray ourselves and our families as having it all together, yet we know this often isn't true. As we cover up reality, dangerous things can happen.

Many years ago, as I was sorting through my own identity, a clear picture came to mind. It was a picture of a heart. The heart wasn't healthy. It had an infection. The infection was growing. Yet it was growing beneath the surface, unexposed but ready to burst at any moment.

Jesus was a part of my life, but I was trying desperately to cover up my insecurities and keep trudging forward. This picture was what I needed to show me the dangers of hiding my pain and weaknesses.

The picture didn't end there. Jesus wanted to expose that infection.

He showed me that if I allowed Him access to open up that infection, it would be messy. But as that infectious material became exposed, I would start to experience healing.

This was the beginning of a new journey in my life of learning to be honest and real before God. I no longer needed to try to act like I had it all together—both to God and others.

It's a journey though, and in every journey there are ups and downs, moments of good health and moments of infections. But if we're being honest with ourselves and with God, He will help us to see when we need to allow Him to expose the pain and start the healing process.

A few key things have helped me in this journey of being real:

- Let God know the real me. Be open in my chats with God (no fancy words needed). Show Him my raw emotions, so that I don't take it out on those I love.
- Find a wise friend I know I can trust. Then be honest with that friend when I'm struggling and ask for prayer, accountability, and guidance. Not all people are trustworthy and not all people will give me good advice, so I must be careful whom I choose.
- Ask for help when I need it. There are times when I've needed a trained counsellor to help guide me. There are times when I've needed family and friends to provide extra support. There are times when I've needed to simplify my schedule to give me the time and space to work through challenging issues.

I encourage you to be courageous by being real. Allow God to have access to those infections in your heart and life in order to start the healing process. Remember that exposing them will be messy at first, but this will allow the healing process to begin.

nineteen

Making Allowance

Read Colossians 3:1–17

By Laurie Pauls

MAKING ALLOWANCE FOR THE FAULTS OF OTHERS, AND forgiving anyone who offends you, are great examples of extending generous grace. I know from fifteen years of marriage and nine years of motherhood that these aren't natural responses to the faults or offences of others.

It takes a conscious effort to have enough allowance ready for even simple things, like my husband throwing hemp hearts in the oatmeal instead of chia seeds, as I had asked. It really is no big deal. But in that moment, it takes self-control, remembering that this is one of those "making allowance moments," and responding in a way that doesn't make it a big deal.

It's quite a bit easier to make allowance for the mistakes of others than it is to make room for the mistakes of those closest to me.

I have one daughter in particular who offends me a lot—and she isn't aware of it, most of the time. To not keep a record of wrongs, extending forgiveness, whether there's an apology or not, has been a challenge and a learning curve for me. Even though she's young and still has a lot of learning and maturing to do, I often find myself feeling resentful and angry. I have a hard time forgiving her.

Children give us many opportunities to learn to forgive, like Jesus asks us to: *"Even if they sin against you seven times in a day and seven times come back to you saying 'I repent,' you must forgive them"* (Luke 17:4, NIV).

In the Gospel of Matthew, the disciple Peter asks how many times he needs to forgive one person who sins against him. Seven times? That sounds generous.

> *Jesus answered, "I tell you, not seven times, but seventy-seven times."*
> —Matthew 18:22, NIV

Before the Holy Spirit convicted me of my need to make more allowance for the faults of others and to forgive more generously, He helped me understand how much allowance He makes for my faults and His extravagant forgiveness for all my sins. In order to make more allowance for others and freely forgive, it helps to experience God's grace personally.

We are all in need of the amazing grace God offers us. As we receive this gift of grace and understand it more fully, we will have more grace to offer those around us.

Listen to the Song:
"Amazing Grace (My Chains Are Gone)," by Chris Tomlin.

twenty

The Butterfly

Read Genesis 1:26–2:7

By Laura Laskowski

Sometimes God is direct in how He speaks to me, but more often He's indirect. Last summer, as I was weeding my garden, the most amazing butterfly landed near me. It completely caught my attention. It was so beautiful.

Then it flew away.

A few minutes passed before this gorgeous butterfly landed beside me again. I thought, *I want to get a picture of this!* So I went to grab my phone from a chair in the shade nearby. Of course, with all that movement, the butterfly flew away.

With my phone in hand, and my camera ready, I said, "Okay, God, this is kind of a crazy request, but if you want me to write about this butterfly, I pray you would bring it back and give me time to take a good picture of it."

As I said this, I felt a little silly in this request of God, but I put it out there anyway.

And guess what? Within a few minutes, that same beautiful butterfly came right back to me… and not only did it come for a moment, it stayed for many, many pictures. I was able to come so close that I could almost touch it!

I was in awe of this moment, and even more in awe of my God who cares so deeply about my heart, what brings me joy, and longs to show me His love for me.

Another curious thing happened after I took these many pictures. The butterfly flew around and around. It kept flying towards the deer fence surrounding the garden and couldn't seem to find its way out.

As I continued on with my weeding, this got me thinking. It felt like God was showing me a picture of myself—a picture of many of us, really. We're like that butterfly, created beautiful and unique with great artistry by God's hand. God has placed us in our garden of life and has provided many, many plants for us.

But weeds also arise within the garden and try to overtake all the beauty and provision God has for us. Without regular maintenance, the weeds will overtake the good plants and literally suck out all the nutrients in the soil, leaving a garden of weeds.

However, with the work of the Gardener, the weeds will be kept at bay; they will still come, but they will not overtake. The plants will grow larger and will soon be strong enough to handle the smaller weeds that creep up beside them.

But remember: the maintenance of weeding, watering, and sunshine are all needed in the garden of life.

So, back to the butterfly. With patience and the help of the Gardener, the butterfly will start to see the plants grow and soon bask in the beauty and provision of the plants and flowers in the garden. It will no longer be looking for a way out, and it will see that the garden which once felt like it was fenced in was actually an amazing garden of goodness, provision, and beauty.

twenty-one

Rescue Plan

Read Jonah 2:1–10

By Laura Laskowski

THE STORY OF JONAH IS BOTH POWERFUL AND FAMILIAR. It tells of his disobedience and God's rescue plan for a man He cherished. As I read this passage today, God spoke to me and reminded me of how He has rescued me from my own belly-of-the-whale experiences.

> *The waters surrounded me, even to my soul; the deep closed around me; weeds were wrapped around my head. I went down to the moorings of the mountains; the earth with its bars closed behind me forever; yet You have brought up my life from the pit, O Lord, my God.*
> —Jonah 2:5–6, NKJV

As we bring children into this world, it feels as though the attack of our enemy intensifies. It could be the lack of sleep, the lack of time to ourselves, the pressure of busyness and materialism, the overwhelming sense of being the parent we so desperately want to be for our kids… or maybe it's all of the above (and more).

Even as my kids get older and I get more sleep, this intensity doesn't seem to disappear, sorry to say. I know grandmothers would agree.

There's a very real battle going on that can't always be directly seen. This is a spiritual battle. Although we can't "see" this battle in our physical world, evidence of it is everywhere.

In this story, the spiritual battle was going on right inside Jonah's heart. He was running away from God and running towards the enemy. God was asking Jonah to love the unlovable, serve the undeserving, and speak God's forgiveness to those who may not listen. Hmmm… does that sound a little like how we might feel as moms? God seems to consistently ask us to keep serving in our homes, keep loving our kids despite their disobedience, and keep giving even when we feel we have nothing left. It kind of makes me want to cry. Maybe even bawl like a baby.

That is so me. I am a *lot* like Jonah at times.

People may not see that in me or even believe it, but God sees it. He knows how disobedient I can be, how angry I can be towards my family, or even how angry I can be in my heart. I can't run from God.

And you know what? You can't either. None of us can. But just like God loved Jonah and creatively rescued him through the belly of a whale, so He will rescue us. As Jonah said, *"Yet You have brought up my life from the pit, O Lord, my God"* (Jonah 2:6, NKJV).

I continue to have up and down days as a mom. There are times when life seems a little easier and times when it feels as though the *"waters surrounded me, even to my soul"* (Jonah 2:5,

NKJV). I am realizing that this is normal and I need not be afraid of it; I need to recognize the spiritual battle that it is.

I'm also learning to quit running from God and start partnering with Him. Together we will be victorious!

twenty-two

Maximizing Our Differences

Read Romans 12:1–16

By Laurie Pauls

OPPOSITES ATTRACT. THEREFORE, THE MAJORITY OF marriages are made up of two very different people. These differences, left to our humanity, have a way of creating great divides. They sometimes lead a couple to think they are actually incompatible.

Jesus said, "[M]y power is made perfect in weakness" (2 Corinthians 12:9, NIV). In our weakness, He is strong. What if we can start to see the differences in our spouse as strength in our weakness? And we are strong in their weaknesses. We are different from each other and have unique ways of viewing the world, so that we can be stronger together.

I am a rescuer and have the unquenchable urge to help or bring relief whenever I can. I can run myself ragged and end up completely miserable because I've carried burdens that weren't mine to carry. My husband, on the other hand, prefers to avoid conflict and has a way of staying out of other people's troubles, trusting that they will figure it out and be stronger for it.

All these years I've allowed this difference to divide us. I've viewed his approach as not caring, as not helping, as lazy. I disagreed with his approach and thought my way was better.

You can see how this difference created a significant wedge between us. This is only one of our many personality differences.

At the moms group I attend, the speaker talked about building endurance and courage in our children. She explained that letting our children go through their struggles plays a crucial role in them developing endurance, courage, and character. Rescuing them can be detrimental to their future and impact the character goals we have for our kids.

All of a sudden, I saw the strength in my husband's approach. With that came affirming thoughts toward him rather than criticism.

It takes self-control and courage to allow those you love to struggle. I can learn so much from my husband and can invite him to help me know when I'm taking my helpful spirit too far... so others can grow strong!

> *Dear brothers and sisters, when troubles of any kind come your way, consider it an opportunity for great joy. For you know that when your faith is tested, your endurance has a chance to grow. So let it grow, for when your endurance is fully developed, you will be perfect and complete, needing nothing.*
>
> —James 1:2–4

My husband and I were created with different personalities, views, and tendencies. The more we can learn to understand, accept, and appreciate our differences, the stronger we will be as a team. Our differences become complements to each other rather than areas of competition. When we put our viewpoints together, we see a fuller picture and therefore make wiser decisions than we would on our own.

Let's learn to love our spouses, with all their differences, in the faithful and incredible ways in which God loves us.

Listen to the Song:
"Reckless Love," by Cory Asbury.

twenty-three

Ski Lesson

Read Psalm 18:28–32

By Laura Laskowski

It's nearing the end of March, so today I went out for likely my last cross-country ski around our property this year.

Overall, I don't love March—I'm so ready for green after many months of winter, and green likely won't show itself for another month. On the flip side, March is often the warmest month of the winter, so the temperature is ideal for outdoor winter sports.

Thus I've been trying to embrace this month and get out and ski either on my own or with my kids. Really, it's a blessing.

As I skied along our now well-worn trail, I reached the garden area. Here I can turn right and take the trail I initially made. It's direct and efficient. Or I can continue straight along the trail my daughter Ashlyn made into the garden. This trail goes up and down, around, through, then up and down again.

The day Ashlyn was the leader in creating this new trail, it drove me crazy to follow her. It felt inefficient. This is quite funny, because I'm typically not an efficient person. For some reason, this dilly-dallying around while we were cross-country skiing just felt frustrating that way. I wanted to actually get some exercise and this was just slowing me down!

So I came to that point in the trail and had to decide which path to take. The first time around, I took the more direct trail, but the second time around I decided to get outside my box and take my daughter's figure-eight trail through the garden.

The next three times, I did the same, going around the figure-eight section of the trail. And guess what? I actually started to enjoy it, because it made me think of Ashlyn and how easily she loves to change the pattern of things. She's a risk-taker, which is clear in her passion for life and sport and activity.

This got me thinking, as I often find I do when I'm out in nature.[4] I so often want my life's path to be direct, clear, obvious, and efficient. And yet it so often feels indirect, unclear, not obvious, and inefficient. There are moments and milestones when I do experience great clarity, but for the most part it feels like I'm doing all these extra figure-eights in the trail.

Today, God reminded me that not only is there purpose in these figure-eights, but there's also incredible need for me to go there. He requires me to go along that crazy, indirect trail to deepen my faith in Him and show me that He's trustworthy. I have to trust because the destination is *not* obvious to me, but to God it's clear as the bright blue sky I see out my window as I write.

---

4 This is one of God's ways of whispering things to me that I need to learn.

God is trustworthy. He will direct my path, no matter what the path looks like. And as I grow in my trust of Him, I will actually start having fun along the way.

twenty-four

He Chose

Read Hebrews 12:1–3, Philippians 2:1–11

By Laurie Pauls

A FEW YEARS AGO, THE HOLY SPIRIT STARTED TEACHING ME to accept the trials and suffering in life instead of resisting them so fiercely. Then this fall, He began teaching me to anticipate and make room for the things in life that don't go the way I want them to go. Now, in the spring, remembering the suffering of Jesus, it amazes me that He chose to suffer. It's one thing to accept and make room for suffering that's forced upon us, but choosing the greatest form of suffering is quite another thing.

> *For the joy set before him he endured the cross, scorning its shame, and sat down at the right hand of the throne of God.*
>
> —Hebrews 12:2, NIV

Jesus knew everything that would happen to Him in Jerusalem, yet He made His way there. This choice wasn't easy for Him, as we can see:

> *"Father, if you are willing, take this cup from me; yet not my will, but yours be done"... And being in anguish, he prayed more earnestly, and his sweat was like drops of blood falling to the ground.*
>
> —Luke 22:42, 44

There was fear, there was dread and anguish, but there was also submission, courage, and obedience. He trusted the plan of the Father and held onto the joy set before Him: rescuing humanity. His suffering and death made a way for us to be God's children, sharing in the amazing gift of a new life that will last forever.

When given a choice, most people choose the road of less suffering. When we do choose suffering, it's for some greater good set before us.

I cannot think of a better example of choosing suffering than motherhood: the heartburn, the stretching muscles, the sore back, the nausea. Then there's the actual labour and delivery, which is one of the most painful experiences one can go through. The suffering and sacrifice don't end there. There's sleepless nights, breastfeeding complications, caring for sick kids, serving them meal after meal and anything else they might need... all with very little appreciation.

Motherhood is a life of sacrifice, for the joy set before us. It's one thing to go into it naively as a first-time mom, not fully understanding what we're getting ourselves into. But most women, given the opportunity, do it all over again, or perhaps another handful of times. It's amazing. This choice to share their body and lay down their life for another, or many others, for the rest of their lives is a beautiful representation of the sacrifice and incredible love of Jesus for us all.

> Listen to the Song:
> "The Passion," by Hillsong.

twenty-five

Twinkle, Twinkle, Big, Big Star
Read Isaiah 40:28–31

By Laura Laskowski

SEVERAL SUMMERS AGO, MY HUSBAND AND KIDS MET MY extended family to go camping for a weekend. I loved watching my three kids interact and play with their cousins.

One morning, my two-year-old son Alex and his three-year-old cousin sat side by side on their tricycles. Their conversation sounded like this:

"This is *my* bike," said my nephew. "It is *big*."

"This is *my* bike," said my son in return. "It is *bigger!*"

My nephew pointed to his dad's truck "That is *my* daddy's truck. It is *big!*"

My son pointed somewhere else. "That is *my* daddy's truck. It is *bigger!*"

"That is *my* dad. He is *big!*"

"That is *my* dad. He is *bigger!*"

And so went their little conversation. It was quite amusing to my brother and me as we listened.

The two cousins held other such conversations over the weekend. They always enjoyed being together despite this aspect of competition between them.

Several days after the camping trip ended, I rocked my boy to sleep while singing to him.

"Twinkle, twinkle, little star…" I began.

My son stopped me abruptly. "No! *Big* star!"

I laughed and tried again. "Twinkle, twinkle, big, big star…"

He smiled and listened quietly as I finished the song with its new lyrics.

For several months after, my son focused on the word *big*. Another song using that word became a favourite: "My God is so big, so strong, and so mighty, there's nothing my God cannot do."

"God is big!" he would say. "He can lift big rocks."

This got me thinking about how true his statement really is. God *is* big and He can lift *big* rocks!

We often live our lives with big rocks in our way, on our shoulders, or in our minds. These rocks prevent us from living out God's purposes in us, from experiencing His blessings. But just as my son reminded me, we have a big God—and He's *my* big God! We can claim Him as our own and He will lift those rocks out of our way. Maybe not in the way we think or expect, but in the way He can best do His work through us and ultimately bless us. Just as He did when Jesus was in the grave. He moved the big rock from the opening and out walked Jesus!

Next time you hear, or even think about, that oh-so-familiar lullaby "Twinkle, Twinkle, Little Star," be reminded of our big God who created that star and wants to do big things in our lives. He is strong enough and big enough to move those rocks, so let's quit trying to do it ourselves.

twenty-six

Your Will Be Done

Read Matthew 6:7–13

By Laurie Pauls

There are days when I don't feel like praying, but I've come to understand these are exactly the times I need to pray. Sometimes my heart is hard toward God or someone else. As soon as I begin to pray, though, a miracle happens in my heart and it softens. When it feels impossible to even open my mouth, the prayer Jesus taught can be either the whole prayer or a jump-start for my prayer.

I've recited the Lord's Prayer hundreds of times in my life. But just the other day, as my husband and I were running and praying it aloud, I received a new understanding from the Holy Spirit of these words: *"your will be done, on earth as it is in heaven"* (Matthew 6:10, NIV).

This statement used to prompt me to pray for more of heaven to come to earth. My spirit would ache for the perfection and glory of heaven to be in this world.

It's not wrong to desire this. In fact, many verses in the Bible describe our spirits groaning for that coming day, because *our citizenship is in heaven. And we eagerly await a Savior from there, the Lord Jesus Christ, who, by the power that enables him to bring everything under his control, will transform our lowly bodies so that they will be like his glorious body.*

—Philippians 3:20–21, NIV

What I came to realize, on that dark and freezing cold morning while we jogged, was that these words acknowledge that God's will is being done here on earth now, just like God's will is done in heaven now. God has authority in heaven above and on the earth below. And right now, while we're waiting for Christ's return, earth will not be like heaven, but that doesn't take away from the fact that God's will is being done in both places.

Jesus said in John 16:33, *"I have told you all this so that you may have peace in me. Here on earth you will have many trials and sorrows. But take heart, because I have overcome the world."*

Through whatever trials and sorrows we may be experiencing, may we cling to the hope and truth that His is the Kingdom, and the power, and the glory, forever!

> Listen to the Song:
> "The Lord's Prayer," by Hillsong.

twenty-seven

Broken for You

Read Jonah 4

By Laurie Pauls

I HAD ANOTHER SUNDAY MORNING, RECENTLY, THAT CLOTHED me in humility before heading to church. It wasn't intentional, but the frustration and anger that burned within me was unstoppable. I wasn't able to stuff it away, turn it off, or breathe through it. Our family drove quietly to church while regret for my actions at home churned within me.

I sat in that pew fully aware of my brokenness, knowing that I was exactly where I needed to be. We sang a song called "Follow You," about following God into the homes of the broken and being used by Him to make His Kingdom come. Instead of feeling perfectly ready to be used by God to help the poor and needy, I knew that my home was a home of the broken, too.

Then, in my brokenness, we were served communion. Never before have I felt that I needed the bread and cup more. I was so thankful I could eat the bread, reminding me that Jesus's body was broken for my brokenness. I was so thankful I could drink the juice, reminding me that Jesus's blood was shed so I could be made whole again. Yes, please! I was consuming the amazing grace, actually accepting and putting into my body the grace poured out for me and for you.

> *Even before he made the world, God loved us and chose us in Christ to be holy and without fault in his eyes. God decided in advance to adopt us into his own family by bringing us to himself through Jesus Christ. This is what he wanted to do, and it gave him great pleasure. So we praise God for the glorious grace he has poured out on us who belong to his dear Son. He is so rich in kindness and grace that he purchased our freedom with the blood of his Son and forgave our sins. He has showered his kindness on us, along with all wisdom and understanding.*
> —Ephesians 1:4–8

As we sang at church, I lifted the words up to God with tears streaming down my face. I knew that through the grace of Jesus, I had been accepted. I am a part of His family. I am His beloved daughter.

I realize that giving all of myself to God includes giving Him the part of me that struggles with anger, self-control, greed, resentment, and self-pity. Just as God was able to use the disobedient and angry Jonah for incredible work in the Kingdom of God, I know that God can use me, His work-in-progress daughter, to walk alongside and bring healing to others who are broken as well.

Listen to the Song:
"Follow You," by Leeland.

twenty-eight

The Oasis
Read John 4:1–26

By Laura Laskowski

Over February break, we often go on a family ski trip. Our kids are now fourteen, ten, and seven, so each year we see progress in their skiing abilities and in our ability as a family to go on long road trips. It's still a big to-do to actually get us all packed up and away from our home for a week, but it's always worth the effort. I love the family time it provides us for a week. The memories made from our family trips are often talked about for months and years to come.

And this year didn't fail to provide memories.

Our first day of travel was a long one—about eleven hours. Five hours in, we were starting to run low on fuel. With our handy GPS, we decided to search for the nearest gas station.

"Okay, we can make it to that next gas station," my husband decided.

Several kilometres later, our GPS stated, "You have arrived at your destination."

Just as my husband was about to turn in, we saw a very abandoned-looking gas station that was perhaps last open a few years prior.

Oh no, I thought to myself.

To make a long ten minutes not sound so long, we continued driving in the hopes that the next gas station would be closer than turning around to the one we had passed earlier.

I started to pray.

Before long, we knew our car was past its limit. I could tell my husband was getting nervous, too.

Somehow—actually I completely know how, since it's all God—we drove over the last hill into the town of Drumheller, Alberta and were able to coast all the rest of the way down to the first gas station. And guess what it was called? The Oasis!

Seriously, no joke. Drive there and you'll see it!

I nearly cried. This gas station was an oasis for us, our car, and our family road trip! It was also a very welcome relief to have a washroom—just one, but at least one—as we had all been holding it for quite some time.

After we had all taken a break and refuelled, we headed back onto the road. My husband and I just had to laugh about the relief we'd felt to make it to that gas station.

As I reflected on this event, I knew God had something to teach me. I was very much reminded of the story of the woman who met Jesus at the well (John 4). She had gone to get water and came away with so much more. Although this woman had been living a life full of poor choices, Jesus had shown love and kindness to her and directed her to the true Oasis—a new life in Christ that would cleanse her from her past behaviour and renew her like nothing else.

Jesus said to her, "[B]ut whoever drinks of the water that I shall give him will never thirst. But the water that I shall give him will become in him a fountain of water springing up into everlasting life" (John 4:14, NKJV).

And how did she respond? In guilt? In shame? In hiding?

No. She said, "*Sir, give me this water, that I may not thirst, nor come here to draw*" (John 4:15).

This is exactly how Jesus wants us to respond to Him. When we're in need, or in doubt, or in fear, or buried in our own poor choices, we can come to Him and He *will* be our Oasis.

Listen to the Song:
"Waterfall," by Chris Tomlin.

twenty-nine

Laughing Ladies
Read Proverbs 31:10–31

By Laurie Pauls

A SON WROTE THE LAST CHAPTER OF PROVERBS ABOUT HIS mother. In it, he reflects on all she had done and all she had been.

Sometimes this passage triggers in me thoughts of not measuring up, but I would encourage you to see yourself through the eyes of your children. They're likely too young to articulate all that they see you do, nor do they appreciate you fully, but they see you working hard, meeting their needs, making decisions for your family, and keeping your fridge and pantry stocked with food. They feel your care for your friends, neighbours, and those who are hurting. They observe you planning ahead and making sure you're prepared for the needs the next season will bring. They hear the wisdom that comes from your experience and watch you take care of your home. As you continue learning to put your trust in God, they will greatly benefit from that as well.

I love how the son describes his mother: *"she laughs without fear of the future"* (Proverbs 31:25). I want to have such a strong hope and steady trust in God that I can laugh without fear of the future.

Most of what will happen in the future is out of our control. It doesn't take much to feel afraid of what might happen.

> *Does it mean he no longer loves us if we have trouble or calamity, or are persecuted, or hungry, or destitute, or in danger, or threatened with death? ...No, despite all these things, overwhelming victory is ours through Christ, who loved us.*
>
> *And I am convinced that nothing can ever separate us from God's love. Neither death nor life, neither angels nor demons, neither our fears for today nor our worries about tomorrow—not even the powers of hell can separate us from God's love. No power in the sky above or in the earth below—indeed, nothing in all creation will ever be able to separate us from the love of God that is revealed in Christ Jesus our Lord.*
>
> —Romans 8:35, 37–39

We can march into the future with hope because we have a good Father in heaven who causes everything to work together for the good of those who love Him (Romans 8:28). We can experience victory in our lives because of Jesus's victory over death when He rose again and returned to heaven to prepare a place for us. We don't need to lose heart over the challenges we face today because we have the Holy Spirit, who is with us through it all, giving us the grace we need.

Laura Laskowski & Laurie Pauls

My purpose in writing is to encourage you and assure you that what you are experiencing is truly part of God's grace for you. Stand firm in this grace.

—1 Peter 5:12

Listen to the Songs:
"Spirit Lead Me," by Influence Music and Michael Ketterer, and "Trust In You," by Lauren Daigle.

thirty

Our Life Mosaic
Read Psalm 5:1–12

By Laura Laskowski

Recently, my daughter Olivia came home with a beautiful project she created in her Industrial Arts class at school. It's a coffee side table. Instead of the table being wooden on top, the teacher had creatively assigned his students to create a mosaic, making each table unique. Carefully they'd broken tiles into smaller pieces and put them together into a design they then glued to the top of their side table.

The results were amazing! Such an interesting way to change up the project and give it that extra punch.

When we brought the table home, the first thing my daughter asked was, "Can you find the one piece that is different in the mosaic?"

At first I tried to just look for a unique shape from the other tiles, but they were all a little different, so that wasn't it. Next, I tried to look for a different colour, but again I couldn't find it.

Then my daughter gave me a hint and said it was white—all the other tiles were either grey, turquoise, or tan-coloured.

Eventually I found it. It was very unassuming, quite small, and really did blend into the whole mosaic despite it being a different colour. I asked my daughter why she had put that one differently coloured tile into the design and she replied that it had been just the right size to fit there.

I like that! No big massive reasoning process needed—the piece just fit!

Being an introvert and a person who relishes in thinking about stuff, sometimes I need to stop trying so hard to fill the hole in my life with so many purposes, ideas, and material things, and just allow the most unassuming and perfectly fitted tile named "Jesus" to fill the space.

Somehow when I do allow Jesus to come in and be a natural part of my life, the whole mosaic of broken pieces comes gently together.

I know that we all have similar needs, or holes, in our lives. We can spend our lives frantically trying to find things to fill those holes. Many of these things can be very well-intentioned. They can be good things—such as being a really good mom, or using our time to serve others, or making a difference in our workplace—but none will fill this one special spot that is meant for Jesus.

God created us to have a relationship with Him, so when we allow His Son Jesus to come into our souls and carry our sins—because, sisters, we all have them—our mosaic will suddenly come together. We'll be walking our day-to-day journey with Jesus beside, in front, and behind us, like that little white piece in the mosaic—white and simple, with no pomp and circumstance, but it makes all the difference.

Draw Near

There's no need to overthink it—just invite and accept Jesus to be a part of your life.

> *For God so loved the world that he gave his one and only Son, that whoever believes in him shall not perish but have eternal life.*
>
> —John 3:16, NIV

Listen to the Song:
"The Table," by Chris Tomlin.

An Invitation

Here's a simple prayer to invite Jesus to become a part of your life if you've never invited Him in. Or, if you do walk with Him and know Him but have felt life stuff overcrowding that space, recommit your heart to Him.

> Dear Jesus,
> I know I have made poor choices in the past. I know I am a sinner. I am sincerely sorry.
> Please forgive me. Today, I want to invite You into my heart and my day-to-day life. Show me how to do this. I believe You died on the cross for me and You rose from the dead so I could have a relationship with God and someday go to heaven. I trust You and I commit myself to following You.
> In Jesus's name, amen.

If you've said this prayer today, I encourage you to tell someone else who follows Jesus—a close friend, a family member, or a church pastor. In this journey, we need other believers and a church family to help support us.

As Laurie and I have shared throughout our writings, our journeys have ups and downs, and we need the support, love, and community of other believers to help us walk it out.

But above all, we need the Bible, God's Word, and the redeeming grace of Jesus. If you just made the choice to join God's amazing family, I can imagine the angels in heaven doing the happy dance!

> *I pray that your love will overflow more and more, and that you will keep on growing in knowledge and understanding. For I want you to understand what really matters, so that you may live pure and blameless lives until the day of Christ's return. May you always be filled with the fruit of your salvation—the righteous character produced in your life by Jesus Christ—for this will bring much glory and praise to God.*
>
> —Philippians 1:9–11

About the Authors

Laurie's Story

A few years ago, my childhood best friend called and said she believed that I needed to start writing. I pondered that for six months before coming to a point of spiritual bankruptcy. I had been trying so hard to fulfill all my roles—wife, mother, Christian, friend, etc.—and continued to fall short. I had to fight hard for hope, joy, and peace. I was exhausted.

C.S. Lewis, in *Mere Christianity*, explains that when we realize we are nothing—that we cannot keep the law, that we cannot earn our salvation or give God anything that wasn't already His in the first place—that is when God can really step in.

I discovered my bankruptcy. I had nothing to give God, and I knew full well that I was broken and messed-up. I knew I couldn't stop messing up.

It was while in this place that I could finally get into a right relationship with God. We discover our bankruptcy by trying—really, really trying—to keep God's law and continually falling on our faces.

As C.S. Lewis wrote, "All this trying leads up to the vital moment at which you turn to God and say, 'You must do this. I can't.'"[5]

It was a moment of healthy bankruptcy where I realized that I needed to stop striving to be better and ask God to transform my heart instead.

The Holy Spirit met me in that place of spiritual bankruptcy and asked me to write every day for a year about the things He was doing in my life. So I obeyed—and I was happy to know where to start with writing!

What the Holy Spirit taught me that year through writing was nothing short of a miracle of transformation in my mind and heart. Of course I'm continually being transformed, but the freedom, healing, and full life I am now living is something I want to share with others. What I share in this book are truths that the Holy Spirit has revealed to me through times of struggle, through His Word, and times of solitude seeking His wisdom as I write.

I have been married to Josh Pauls for fifteen years. Being married at age twenty, I had a lot of maturing to do, and I'm so thankful for his steady faithfulness to me. His love, patience, and acceptance of all that I am has been the greatest gift he could give me.

I have two daughters, Kaylin and Raya. God knew they were exactly what I needed in order to learn, grow, and find myself needing God in my day-to-day life. Motherhood has brought

---

5 C.S. Lewis, *Mere Christianity* (New York, NY: HarperCollins, 1980), 146.

endless amounts of goodness, but it has also shone a spotlight on all my fears, weaknesses, and failures. They humble me and keep me seeking God for wisdom, help, hope, peace, and joy.

If you don't find me in the kitchen making meals, taking my girls to activities, or volunteering my time, you will find me running with my dog, reading a book in the sun, or snuggled up on the couch taking a power nap.

Laura's Story

First and foremost, I am so thankful to be a child of God. I grew up in a wonderful family of six kids in which my parents deeply instilled the importance of faith in Jesus. I've been married to my very committed and loving husband Kevin for more than twenty years! We have three children whom we're trying our best to raise in the manner Jesus calls us to. We live on an acreage in the beautiful farming country of Saskatchewan where I love to garden, cross-country ski, write, and have campfires with my family.

Marriage and mothering have been God's greatest refining tools in my life. I've had to learn and relearn to base the core of my significance on how Jesus sees me. On my many days of feeling incapable and unworthy of this call to be a parent and wife, Jesus gives me strength, hope, mercy, wisdom, and love to keep trekking ahead.

In the weeks when I'm too busy to sit and read my Bible, I start to suffer. My thoughts drift to unhealthy places, my body grows weary, and my soul empties. I have realized my incredible need and dependence on Jesus.

In my early years of being a mom and wife, I came to a place where I was desperate for hope. Desperate for energy. Desperate for purpose and significance.

Very gently and gradually, Jesus renewed each of these within me. He often did this by speaking intentionally to me through simple daily tasks and happenings in my roles as wife and mother. I began to write these down. Soon I started to feel the deep joy of wanting to share these words. I felt an immense desire to help others through similar experiences.

Over the years, this desire to write has grown and expanded—and now it is very exciting to be along on this ride as God takes my stories and lessons into the homes and hearts of other families. I pray they will give you a new sense of hope and joy in your calling to live out the day to day of your life. God loves you and wants to be invited to walk alongside you.

> *Yet I will rejoice in the LORD! I will be joyful in the God of my salvation! The Sovereign LORD is my strength! He makes me as surefooted as a deer, able to tread upon the heights.*
>
> —Habakkuk 3:18–19

Visit us at
www.messagesforher.com